Foreword

Teara Booker is on a mission to help women live healthy lives in mind, body and especially soul. **THE WELL WOMAN JOURNAL** is her latest purposeful offering with hopes to assist women in finding their center of peace. Unlike other journaling books, Teara's journal helps women to focus on the 9 important dimensions of wellness through writing prompts, quotes and other tools, providing them an opportunity to explore the root causes of the things that may be blocking them from their peace. The journey women will take through THE WELL WOMAN JOURNAL will be soul-stirring and life-affirming.

~ Candance L. Greene Author of *Inhale Peace: A 31-Day Journey to Realign with God's Peace*

This journal belongs to:

_____

This Journal is For You...

- If you want to get organized
- If you want to set goals
- If you want to declutter, organize, schedule or plan.
- If you want to observe growth.
- If you want to be creative.
- If you like to track important things.
- If you want to take time for yourself.
- If you want to budget and save
- If you want to think BIG
- If you are ready to LIVE WELL!

The Well Woman

A Guide to Explore the 9 Dimensions of Wellness

About the Author

Teara Q. Booker is an innovative health and wellness professional with a focus on educating, coaching, training, and supporting women and families. Ms. Booker is a lifelong learner and entrepreneur. She has a toolbox of skills and talents that she has been able to use to empower, support others, and generate income for her family.

Currently, Ms. Booker is a professor, social entrepreneur, and wellness practitioner. She teaches business, health, and wellness courses at several institutions of higher learning. Ms. Booker is the owner of Well With Her Soul, where her overall mission was formed. Teara is passionate about wellness, happiness, and peace. She believes all people are entitled to live a mindful and content life. She is a mother, a certified yoga instructor, author, certified wellness and v-steam practitioner, and life coach.

Ms. Booker is also the founder of Y.A.M: Yoga, Artistic Expression, and Mindfulness, where she works to make the connection between artistic expression, mindfulness, and daily yoga practice for black children and families.

Website: www.wellwithhersoul.com
IG: @wellwithhersoul_
FB: Well With Her Soul

12 Tips to Get Started with Journaling

- Get a Journal
- Journal in the morning or at Night
- Secure a Dedicated Space
- Set a Reminder
- Set a Timer
- Free Write
- Use Journal Prompts
- Ask Yourself Questions
- Don't Put Limits or Restrictions on Journaling
- Make Lists
- Carry Your Journal with You
- Enjoy It!

Emotional Wellness

#AWellWoman

Emotional Wellness inspires self-care, relaxation, stress reduction and the development of inner strength. It is important to be attentive to both positive and negative feelings and be able to understand how to handle these emotions.

If you look at what you have in life, you'll always have more. If you look at what you don't have in life, you'll never have enough.

- *Oprah Winfrey*

#AWellWoman

List 20 things that make you smile.

Affirmation:
I am love, I am peace,
I am _____

I am in total control of my destiny.

Date _____

Emotional Check-In

Calm	Surprised	Bored	Hurt
Content	Startled	Cranky	Disappointed
Satisfied	Unsure	Distracted	Sad
Relaxed	Apprehensive	Aggravated	Distraught
Happy	Afraid	Angry	Grief
Giddy	Confused	Frustrated	Depressed
Interested	Nervous	Distaste	Distracted
Enthusiastic		Disbelief	Despair
Overjoyed	Anxious	Disgusted	Irate
Excited	Terrified		
Amazed		Apathetic	Bitter
Thrilled	Frantic	Contemptuous	Loathing
Fixated	Hysterical	Disdain	Enraged
Exuberant			
Obsessed			

Today, I am feeling _____ *because* _____

_____

_____

_____

Date _____

Emotional Check-In

Calm	Surprised	Bored	Hurt
Content	Startled	Cranky	Disappointed
Satisfied	Unsure	Distracted	Sad
Relaxed	Apprehensive	Aggravated	Distraught
Happy	Afraid	Angry	Grief
Giddy	Confused	Frustrated	Depressed
Interested	Nervous	Distaste	Distracted
Enthusiastic		Disbelief	Despair
Overjoyed	Anxious	Disgusted	Irate
Excited	Terrified		
Amazed		Apathetic	Bitter
Thrilled	Frantic	Contemptuous	Loathing
Fixated	Hysterical	Disdain	Enraged
Exuberant			
Obsessed			

Today, I am feeling _____ *because* _____

_____

_____

_____

Date _____

Emotional Check-In

Calm	Surprised	Bored	Hurt
Content	Startled	Cranky	Disappointed
Satisfied	Unsure	Distracted	Sad
Relaxed	Apprehensive	Aggravated	Distraught
Happy	Afraid	Angry	Grief
Giddy	Confused	Frustrated	Depressed
Interested	Nervous	Distaste	Distracted
Enthusiastic		Disbelief	Despair
Overjoyed	Anxious	Disgusted	Irate
Excited	Terrified		
Amazed		Apathetic	Bitter
Thrilled	Frantic	Contemptuous	Loathing
Fixated	Hysterical	Disdain	Enraged
Exuberent			
Obsessed			

Today, I am feeling _____ *because* _____

_____

_____

_____

Date _____

Emotional Check-In

Calm	Surprised	Bored	Hurt
Content	Startled	Cranky	Disappointed
Satisfied	Unsure	Distracted	Sad
Relaxed	Apprehensive	Aggravated	Distraught
Happy	Afraid	Angry	Grief
Giddy	Confused	Frustrated	Depressed
Interested	Nervous	Distaste	Distracted
Enthusiastic		Disbelief	Despair
Overjoyed	Anxious	Disgusted	Irate
Excited	Terrified	Apathetic	Bitter
Amazed			
Thrilled	Frantic	Contemptuous	Loathing
Fixated	Hysterical	Disdain	Enraged
Exuberant			
Obsessed			

Today, I am feeling _____ because _____

_____

_____

_____

Power is not given to you. You have to take it.

- Beyoncé Knowles

How will you change the things you are unhappy with in the next 3-6 months?

Intellectual Wellness

#AWellWoman

Intellectual Wellness encourages us to engage in creative and mentally-stimulating activities. These activities should expand your knowledge and skills while allowing you to share your knowledge and skills with others. Intellectual wellness can be developed through academics, cultural involvement, community involvement and personal hobbies.

Words have power. TV has power. My pen has power.

- Shonda Rhimes

 Affirmation:

I will not compare myself to others because I am my only competition!

What is the driving force in my life? (e.g. My why, reason for showing up, etc.)

What are your three professional development priorities right now? Pick one to discuss in detail.

How will you be more creative this month, week, or year?

Affirmations:

I am the most intelligent person on the planet.

I am great at solving problems.

I will concentrate and focus fully.

THOUGHT TRACKER

MOOD

TRIGGER

IMMEDIATE THOUGHTS

RATIONAL THOUGHTS

ACTION & GOAL

MOOD

THOUGHT TRACKER

MOOD

TRIGGER

IMMEDIATE THOUGHTS

RATIONAL THOUGHTS

ACTION & GOAL

MOOD

THOUGHT TRACKER

MOOD

TRIGGER

IMMEDIATE THOUGHTS

RATIONAL THOUGHTS

ACTION & GOAL

MOOD

THOUGHT TRACKER

MOOD

TRIGGER

IMMEDIATE THOUGHTS

RATIONAL THOUGHTS

ACTION & GOAL

MOOD

The most common way people give up their power is by thinking they don't have any.

− Alice Walker

How will you be more creative this month, week, or year?

Social Wellness

#AWellWoman

Social Wellness relates to the relationships we have and how we interact with others. Our relationships can offer support during difficult times. Social wellness involves building healthy, nurturing and supportive relationships as well as fostering a genuine connection with those around you.

Just try new things. Don't be afraid. Step out of your comfort zones and soar, all right?

— *Michelle Obama*

If you could do something from your past again, how would you do it differently?

Travel Bucket List

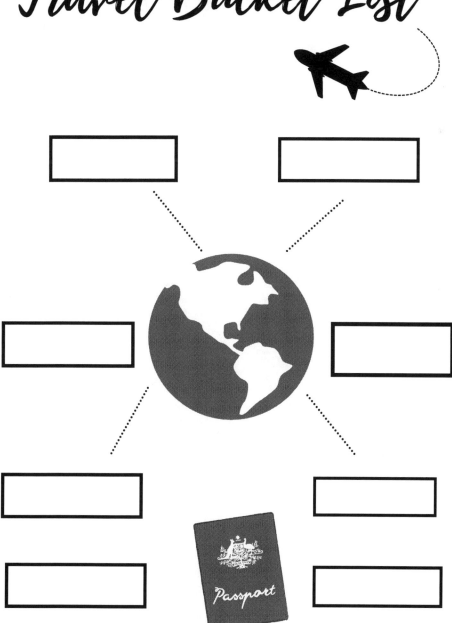

Travel Bucket List

It is good to go out alone from time to time. Describe the ideal solo date. This could be in the states or abroad.

You wanna fly, you got to give up the thing that weighs you down.

— Toni Morrison

Birthdays

| January | February | March |

| April | May | June |

Birthdays

| July | August | September |

| October | November | December |

Physical and Fitness Wellness

#AWellWoman

Physical Wellness promotes proper care of our bodies for optimal health and functioning. There are many elements of physical wellness that all must be cared for together. Overall physical wellness encourages the balance of physical activity, nutrition and mental well-being to keep your body in top condition.

The Five W's in Wellness

Who you are is what makes you special. Do not change for anyone.

What lies ahead will always be a mystery. Do not be afraid to explore.

When life pushes you over, you push back harder.

Where there are choices to make, make the one you won't regret.

Why things happen will never be certain. Take it in stride and move forward.

Just believe in yourself! Even if you don't, pretend that you do, and at some point, you will!

—Venus Williams

What is one thing I can do daily, weekly, and monthly to improve my health?

If fitness came in a bottle, everyone would have a great body!

- Cher

Affirmations:

I am healthy, happy, and fine as ever!

I appreciate and love myself unconditionally.

What would you attempt if you knew you could not fail?

Financial Wellness

#AWellWoman

Financial Wellness involves the process of learning how to successfully manage financial expenses. Money plays a critical role in our lives and not having enough of it impacts health as well as academic performance. Financial stress is repeatedly found to be a common source of stress, anxiety and fear for adults.

What is your attitude towards money?

Affirmations:

I attract money.

My accomplishments are out of this world!

I am proud of my efforts.

I am liberated and financially free.

What does retirement look like? Be very descriptive.

What will your financial life look like in 5-10 years?

The only way you will ever permanently take control of your financial life is to dig deep and fix the root problem.

- Suze Orman

Savings Tracker

20	40	60	80	100	**YAY**
120	140	160	180	200	**AWESOME**
220	240	260	280	300	**HELL YEAH**
320	340	360	380	400	**HOLY CRAP**
420	440	460	480	500	**OMG**
520	540	560	580	600	**SWEET**
620	640	660	680	700	**WAY TO GO**
720	740	760	780	800	**SUPER**
820	840	860	880	900	**KICK ASS**
920	940	960	980	1000	**HOLY SHIT**

Debt Payoff Tracker

20	40	60	80	100	**YAY**
120	140	160	180	200	**AWESOME**
220	240	260	280	300	**HELL YEAH**
320	340	360	380	400	**HOLY CRAP**
420	440	460	480	500	**OMG**
520	540	560	580	600	**SWEET**
620	640	660	680	700	**WAY TO GO**
720	740	760	780	800	**SUPER**
820	840	860	880	900	**KICK ASS**
920	940	960	980	1000	**HOLY SHIT**

Savings Tracker

20	40	60	80	100	**YAY**
120	140	160	180	200	**AWESOME**
220	240	260	280	300	**HELL YEAH**
320	340	360	380	400	**HOLY CRAP**
420	440	460	480	500	**OMG**
520	540	560	580	600	**SWEET**
620	640	660	680	700	**WAY TO GO**
720	740	760	780	800	**SUPER**
820	840	860	880	900	**KICK ASS**
920	940	960	980	1000	**HOLY SHIT**

Debt Payoff Tracker

20	40	60	80	100	**YAY**
120	140	160	180	200	**AWESOME**
220	240	260	280	300	**HELL YEAH**
320	340	360	380	400	**HOLY CRAP**
420	440	460	480	500	**OMG**
520	540	560	580	600	**SWEET**
620	640	660	680	700	**WAY TO GO**
720	740	760	780	800	**SUPER**
820	840	860	880	900	**KICK ASS**
920	940	960	980	1000	**HOLY SHIT**

Occupational Wellness

#AWellWoman

Occupational wellness inspires us to prepare for work in which we will gain personal satisfaction and find enrichment in our life. Your attitude about work is a crucial influence for occupational development. Occupational wellness allows you to explore various career options and encourages you to pursue the opportunities you enjoy the most. This can also include entrepreneurship.

I am lucky that whatever fear I have inside me, my desire to win is always stronger.

- Serena Williams

What has been your biggest accomplishment over the last three months and what do you wish to do better over the next 90 days?

In what ways can I be transformed?

Affirmations:

I will keep a positive attitude in the workplace no matter what.

I can, I will, I must.

I birth new ideas in my sleep.
You are unstoppable.

Motivation comes to me easily and I also successfully motivate others.

Discuss a big decision that frightened you initially, but paid off in the end.

Sometimes you've got to let everything go – purge yourself. If you are unhappy with anything, whatever it is bringing you down, get rid of it!

— Tina Turner

My Daily Hustle

Date: _____

Today I'm Hustling Because

○ _____

○ _____

○ _____

My Schedule

6 _____
7 _____
8 _____
9 _____
10 _____
11 _____
12 _____
1 _____
2 _____
3 _____
4 _____
5 _____
6 _____
7 _____
8 _____

3 Things I Am Committed To Getting Done Today:

_____

_____

_____

My To-Dos

○ _____
○ _____
○ _____

Notes

My Daily Hustle

Date: _____

Today I'm Hustling Because

○ _____

○ _____

○ _____

My Schedule

6 _____
7 _____
8 _____
9 _____
10 _____
11 _____
12 _____
1 _____
2 _____
3 _____
4 _____
5 _____
6 _____
7 _____
8 _____

3 Things I Am Committed To Getting Done Today:

_____

_____

_____

My To-Dos

○ _____
○ _____
○ _____

Notes

My Daily Hustle

Date: _____

Today I'm Hustling Because

◯ _____

◯ _____

◯ _____

My Schedule

6 _____
7 _____
8 _____
9 _____
10 _____
11 _____
12 _____
1 _____
2 _____
3 _____
4 _____
5 _____
6 _____
7 _____
8 _____

3 Things I Am Committed To Getting Done Today:

_____

_____

_____

My To-Dos

◯ _____
◯ _____
◯ _____

Notes

My Daily Hustle

Date: _____

Today I'm Hustling Because

○ _____

○ _____

○ _____

My Schedule

6 _____
7 _____
8 _____
9 _____
10 _____
11 _____
12 _____
1 _____
2 _____
3 _____
4 _____
5 _____
6 _____
7 _____
8 _____

3 Things I Am Committed To Getting Done Today:

_____

_____

_____

My To-Dos

○ _____
○ _____
○ _____

Notes

Spiritual Wellness

#AWellWoman

Spiritual Wellness allows us to be in tune with our spiritual side. This realm of wellness lets us find meaning in life events and define our individual purpose. Spiritual wellness can be defined through various factors including religious faith, values, ethics and morals. Regardless of whether you believe in a particular religious faith, there is always something to be learned about how you see yourself in the world.

It isn't until you come to a spiritual understanding of who you are – not necessarily a religious feeling, but deep down, the spirit within – that you can begin to take control.

— Oprah Winfrey

What is my calling in life?

Affirmations:

Good things take time.

Prayer changes things.

Each day I am born again, so what I do today is the only thing that matters.

There comes a time when time itself is ready for a change.

— Coretta Scott King

This day | week | month, I was most blessed by _____

Daily Mindfulness

My Intention Today _____

_____

_____

Today I will be mindful when:	
Walking	○
Eating	○
Driving	○
Exercising	○
Resting	○

Meditation

Time:

Duration:

Comment:

Daily Gratitude

Hourly Meditation Moments

_____
_____
_____
_____
_____
_____
_____
_____
_____
_____
_____
_____
_____
_____
_____
_____

Daily Mindfulness

My Intention Today _____

_____

_____

Today I will be mindful when:

- Walking ○
- Eating ○
- Driving ○
- Exercising ○
- Resting ○

Meditation

Time:

Duration:

Comment:

Daily Gratitude

Hourly Meditation Moments

_____
_____
_____
_____
_____
_____
_____
_____
_____
_____
_____
_____
_____
_____
_____
_____

Daily Mindfulness

My Intention Today _____

_____

_____

Today I will be mindful when:	
Walking	○
Eating	○
Driving	○
Exercising	○
Resting	○

Meditation

Time:

Duration:

Comment:

Daily Gratitude

Hourly Meditation Moments

_____
_____
_____
_____
_____
_____
_____
_____
_____
_____
_____
_____
_____
_____
_____

Daily Mindfulness

My Intention Today _____

_____

Today I will be mindful when:

- Walking ○
- Eating ○
- Driving ○
- Exercising ○
- Resting ○

Meditation

Time:

Duration:

Comment:

Daily Gratitude

Hourly Meditation Moments

_____
_____
_____
_____
_____
_____
_____
_____
_____
_____
_____
_____
_____
_____
_____

Sexual Wellness

#AWellWoman

Sexual Wellness is a state of physical, mental and social well-being in relation to sexuality. It requires a positive and respectful approach to sexuality and sexual relationships, as well as the possibility of having pleasurable and safe sexual experiences, free of coercion, discrimination and violence.

Sex with the right person can be addictive so choose wisely!

Perfect is Boring.

— *Tyra Banks*

What is one thing I can do this month to please myself and / or my partner?

Affirmations:

I am a great lover.

My sexual confidence is growing.

Sex is not a dirty word!

If time froze for everyone but you for one hour, who would you like to see naked?

Relationship Building

My Future Partner's Qualities

The top five qualities I want in a partner:

_____

_____

_____

_____

_____

The top five dealbreakers in a partner:

_____

_____

_____

_____

_____

How to love me:

_____

_____

_____

_____

_____

Relationship Building

My Curent Partner's Qualities

The top five qualities I love about my partner:

_____
_____
_____
_____
_____

My partner's love languages:

_____
_____
_____
_____

How my partner shows me love:

_____
_____
_____
_____
_____

Environmental Wellness

#AWellWoman

Environmental wellness inspires us to live a lifestyle that is respectful of our surroundings. It encourages us to live in harmony with the earth by taking action. It is our responsibility to promote and encourage interaction with nature as often as possible.

The progress of the world will call for the best that all of us have to give.

- Mary McLeod Bethune

What are 5 new things you can discover and 1 of those things you can commit to and why?

Affirmations:

I will make my space healthy.

I am right where I need to be.

I live a purposeful and prosperous life.

The 2 moments I will never forget in life are....describe them in great detail and include what makes them so unforgettable.

What's the world for if you can't make it up the way you want it?

— Toni Morrison

DECLUTTER SCHEDULE

CLEAR THE COAT CLOSET. GET RID OF OLD CLOTHES AND DONATE TO CHARITY.	ORGANIZE THE PANTRY.	FOLD, STRAIGTHEN AND DONATE ITEMS FROM THE LINEN CLOSET.
CLEAN OUT YOUR REFRIGERATOR.	CLEAR THE BOOKSHELF, KEEP BOOKS AND DITCH THE REST.	CATCH UP ON YOUR MAIL.
SWEEP AND CLEAN THE PORCHES.	TACKLE THE KIDS ROOMS.	FOLD AND PUT AWAY EVERYTHING IN THE LAUNDRY ROOM.
CLEAN YOUR SHOWER FROM TOP TO BOTTOM.	GO THROUGH ALL OF THE DRAWERS IN YOUR HOME, INCLUDING DESKS.	CELEBRATE, YOU HAVE DECLUTTERED IT ALL !

# Notes

 # Notes

Made in the USA
Middletown, DE
15 April 2024